FREEDOM'S WALL

FREEDOM'S WALL

Bruce Robertson

Freedom's Wall
Copyright © 2020 by Bruce Robertson

Library of Congress Control Number: 2019919088
ISBN-13:   Paperback: 978-1-64749-008-9
            ePub: 978-1-64749-009-6

American Poetry

All rights reserved. No part of this publication may be reproduced, distributed, or transmitted in any form or by any means, including photocopying, recording, or other electronic or mechanical methods, without the prior written permission of the publisher or author, except in the case of brief quotations embodied in critical reviews and certain other noncommercial uses permitted by copyright law.

Although every precaution has been taken to verify the accuracy of the information contained herein, the author and publisher assume no responsibility for any errors or omissions. No liability is assumed for damages that may result from the use of information contained within.

Printed in the United States of America

GoToPublish LLC
1-888-337-1724
www.gotopublish.com
info@gotopublish.com

CONTENTS

DISCLAIMER VII
DEDICATIONS IX
    FREEDOM'S WALL 1
    LOST HEROES OF THE WAR 2
    A SPECIAL WALL 3
    NOT FAMILIES ANYMORE 4
    THE NAMES UPON THE WALL 5
    A VETERAN 6
    A MASTERPIECE FOR FREEDOM 7
    VETERANS AND WARRIORS 8
    A FIGURE 9
    IF 10
    A STREAM OF SOLDIERS 11
    AMEN! 12
    NO MATTER! 13
    A SOLDIER'S LULLABY 14
    SOLOMON'S BLUFF 15
    MY TOWN 16
    THE UNSEEN SHADOWS OF YESTERDAY 17
    THINGS IN COMMON 18
    THE WALL WITH A PITFALL 19
    SIXTY THOUSAND NAMES 20
    UNCLE JED 21
    THE WALL 22
    THE DISAPPEARING MAN 23
    THE SOLDIER 24
    FREEDOM AND LIBERTY 25
    LIBERTY FOR EVERYONE 26
    THE WALL WILL LAST 27

CHRISTMAS POEMS 29
   SANTA? 31
   RUDOLPH, RUDOLPH 32
   I'M PROUD 34
   SANTA'S FAST ASLEEP 36
   SANTA SNORES! 37
   SANTA'S SURPRISE 38
   Where's Rudolph 40
   Runaway Deer! 41
   Christmas Greetings 42
   CHRISTMAS AGAIN 43
   A VERY SPECIAL MOMENT 44
   KEEPING CHRISTMAS CHRISTMAS 45
   THE CHRISTMAS TREE 46
   Santa Being Santa 47
   Arnie 48
   Lessons 50
   Losing Weight 51
   Mrs. Clause 52
   No Christmas! 53
   The Mission 54
   Ready To Deliver 55
   Santa's Glasses 56
   Santa's Everywhere! 57
   Santa's Getting Old 58
   The Brotherhood 60
   The Letter 61
   The Christmas Party 62
   The Coffee Caper 63
   The Wall 64
   The Tooth Ache 65
   The Toast 66
   What about Santa 67
   Where Have You Been 68
   Two Bosom Buddies 69
   Christmas Morning 70
   The Bible 71

DISCLAIMER

I'm not a veteran, but I have three uncles that were. These poems are based on things I was told by them. All my poems were based on Vietnam vetrans I have met.

The characters in my poems are fictional. They represent all vetrans who have passed in warfare.

All rights reserved. No parts of this book may be reproduced in any manner or form whatsoever, without the expressed written permission of the author.

DEDICATIONS

I dedicate these poems to all soldiers who lost their lives defending our country, their families who are the true victims of war. Not only those who lost their lives, but the unscaved and maimed who sacrificed their freedom so others can have a better life; to all soldiers gone and still alive. Thank You!

I would also like to thank my wife Karen who has stood behind me in my endeavors. Jan Jacob who typed out my poems, Sonia Gibbs who kept my emotions on an even keel, Carl Banks Jr. who encouraged me all the way, Mr. Dee Butler who put it all together and most of all God who blessed me with spiritual guidance.

Thank You
Bruce Robertson

FREEDOM'S WALL

Every name on Freedom's Wall
Is a hero rich with pride,
Who fought for peace and justice,
Who laughed, who wept, who died
Who presented commitment --
The greatest gift of all --
There for everyone to see
Etched on Freedom's Wall.

Though they've gone to Heaven,
In loved ones' hearts they dwell.
In memories they linger.
In courage they excel -- Excel in being heroes,
In answering freedom's call.
Countless men and women
Now on Freedom's Wall.

So give credence to these hero's
Who won us liberty,
Sacrificing everything
Just so we'd be free.
They took the final journey giving us their all
With honor and with spirit –
Now on Freedom's Wall.

LOST HEROES OF THE WAR

The wall meets the ground, then sinks
Into the earth.
It was put together with loving hands and
Blessed for all its worth.

Americans united with a common goal:
To honor those who've lost their lives
Individually and whole.

Loved ones won't be coming home
They remain deep in families' hearts.
They want to be close to them,
Though they're far apart.

Families come, then walk away
To return again once more
To the wall that honors soldiers,
Lost heroes of the war.

A SPECIAL WALL

People pass me every day. They don't ever hear me call.
They never stop and take a look! I'm a very special wall!

I have the names of heroes who've fought and died
Fighting for freedom and a chance to stay alive.

I think I deserve a look. I'm not hard to find.
If you take a little while, I may be worth your time.

ALL the soldiers on the wall would love to have you stay.
Thank you, heroes every one for what you do each day.

NOT FAMILIES ANYMORE

A family came to the wall and the boy began to cry.
He looked up at his mother and asked, "Why did daddy die?"
The Mother just shook her hard . . . "for our nation's sake."
The little boy just stood there. It was more than he could take.

The family turned and walked away.
A tear came to my eye
I see this almost every day.
It's enough to make you cry.

Every name on the wall is a tragedy of war.
And the families of these soldiers are not families anymore.

THE NAMES UPON THE WALL

I came upon the wall, so beautiful to see.
But the names upon the wall weren't who thought they'd be.

I thought they'd be legends whom everybody knew,
Not unknown soldiers who died for me and you.

And when I saw how many, it nearly blew my mind -
Almost sixty thousand, gone for all of time!

I shook my head. "Oh, well . . . it's sad, but golly gee -
What have all these names have to do with me?"

The answer, I guess, is that they answered the call.
I was never patriotic until I came upon the wall.

A VETERAN

A soldier just home from battle visits Freedom's Wall.
He has mixed feelings about fighting there at all.

He knows that fighting battles is a necessary thing.
He also knows the trauma and the heartache it can bring.

He stares at the names. You can tell he really cares.
He also realizes that his name is not up there.

But he's done his tour of duty,
He'd answered freedom's call.

All his fighting buddies,
Their names are on the wall.

He turns and walks away; a tear rolls from his eye.
He feels kind of silly - a soldier never cries!

The wall has a certain calling for veterans such as he.
He salutes the wall and the men who fought to keep us free.

A MASTERPIECE FOR FREEDOM

A masterpiece for freedom, a monument of love –
Understanding what it's like to have something you're proud of.

To honor those in combat who bravely lost their lives:
A tribute to their families: their sons, daughters, and wives.

Memories of yesterday and how it is right now -
The bittersweet, the agony and the heartache it allows

All this comes together and makes us stand up tall –
Proud to be Americans with the names there upon the wall.

VETERANS AND WARRIORS

Veterans who visit the wall are warriors through and through.
They love their country with all their hearts, their loyalty true.

They fought with strength and honor, dignity and pride.
That's why they visit the wall. That's where their hearts reside.

They salute the flag with pride and touch the wall with love -
Dedicated soldiers, blessed by God above.

This sets them apart from what they achieved.
The names upon the wall is the reason they believe.

Some are names of sons and daughters.
Others are their friends.

They all have death in common.
That's where freedom bends.

It takes a hero's passing for people to react.
That's what freedom means to them: forever looking back.

A FIGURE

When the lights came on, a figure was
Standing at the wall -
A very lonely figure, statuesque and tall.

He just stood there motionless
Like a picture in a frame -
Standing at the wall and staring
At a very special name.

Ten years later, when all was quiet,
The man returned again.
He just stood there at the wall
With his head slightly bent.

He finally spoke in a whisper,
After all was said and done . . .
Thirty years ago this day, he said he lost his only son.

IF

If people could just get along, there wouldn't be any wall
- Nothing to obstruct us, no barriers at all.

Human life would be valuable, more valuable than gold.
The miracle of life would be something to behold.

We would be forever what we were supposed to be:
Children of our Creator living in harmony.

If people would accept the fact nobodies the same
And let everyone existing be merciful and tame,

Then maybe, just maybe, everyone could stand up tall
And the wall with solders' names would not be there at all.

A STREAM OF SOLDIERS

On a certain day each year you can see a steady stream
Of soldiers lost in battles coming down from heaven's beam

And disappearing into the wall -- sixty thousand names:
Loved ones gone forever in the wall where they will reign.

Now there's just a memory of long lost years before:
Someone remembers them before they went to war:

A laugh, a joke, a remembrance - a special time of day
Now imprisoned in cement, eternally displayed.

I hope and pray there'll be a time when war will not exist, When
families and loved ones can bask in happiness.

And the wall will be remembered at a time so long ago –
When freedom had been paid for by the ones that we loved so.

AMEN!

The pastor spoke a special prayer for the soldiers on the wall. He said, "Father keep them with you. "
They answered freedom's call.

They're heroes in their own right."
They kept our country safe.
In time evil will disappear - gone without a trace.
Everyone was silent. The pastor was the best.
He continued with his prayer until it manifest.

I know you hear me, Jesus. I know my time must end.
Then sixty thousand soldiers, together, proudly said , "AMEN!"

NO MATTER!

No matter what you do, no matter how you feel,
Not everyone is interested in what you yield.

Some just hem and haw; others walk away.
Still others are kind enough to stay.

That's the way it is about the wall that some have built:
Folks were kind enough to tell us how they felt:

How they feel about heroes and what they have to do.
And dying for their country - how tragic that is, too.

No matter the swagger that people may have -
Some nonchalant and others simply sad,

It doesn't make much difference in the end.
The Freedom Wall will still be there to honor and defend.

A SOLDIER'S LULLABY

A lady with a child walked up to the wall
And whispered softly a lullaby
The prettiest of them all.

I walked up and said, "That's beautiful!
I've never heard it before."

"I know. My husband wrote it before he went to war."

I looked around. "Where is he? I'd like to shake his
hand." She smiled and pointed to the wall:
"Right there," she said so grand.

"Number twenty-two: Sergeant Leonard Brown.
He was killed twenty years ago."

I never made a sound. I felt a tear in my eye.
I said to her, "I'm so sorry!"

She said, "Don't be sorry!
Before he went away, he said to me,
'Let's treasure every moment for I'll be home someday.'"

SOLOMON'S BLUFF

When a soldier is tired and he has gone the extra mile,
He wants to relax and rest his eyes a while.

Where does he go just to get away?
Solomon's Bluff, off of Mythical Anabel Bay.

The water is warm; the sand is fine.
The perfect place to cast your line.

There's no strife, no enemy -
Just lay back and enjoy the scenery!

It's a mythical place where soldiers go -
Away from harm. It's good to know

There is a place to get away.
Solomon's Bluff, off of Mythical Anabel Bay.

MY TOWN

I've been away for six years and now I'm finally home.
In the same rustic town where I lived alone.

The town I lived in years ago is not the same at all.
The corner bar at Elm and Main is now a city mall.

The people that I used to know have mostly gone away.
Some went to fight a foreign war; others simply strayed.

Even though I was born here, it's really not the same.
It's funny what time can do even though I'm not to blame.

You can always go back to the place but not back in time.
Nothing stays the same, except in your mind.

You accept life's changes and live from day to day –
As boring as it seems, that's the only way.

THE UNSEEN SHADOWS OF YESTERDAY

The unseen shadows of yesterday
Are the families of those who died.
Seldom seen . . . forgotten, and left for those who cry. . .

Those who suffer from memories of how it was before
When they laughed and joked with their loved ones
Before they went to war.

Now they're hovering in the past, trapped and left to weep –
Trying to relive the past and often losing sleep.
Just an hour longer is all they require
To bring back yesterday and relight that inner fire.

That's why it's important to voice what's in their soul,
To cry when they feel like crying
When they're about to lose control.

Their emotions and their passions
Are the key to what they say.
For the tomorrows become the yesterdays
That sadly got away.

THINGS IN COMMON

On The Freedom Wall are many, many soldier's names – Sixty
thousand individuals with different claims to fame.

One was a singer of many country western tunes.
Another was an artist who drew well-known cartoons.

Another soldier whom I knew went to school with me.
We graduated together in the class of nineteen sixty-three.

He wanted to be a writer, a novelist by trade.
He did the very best he could but never made the grade.

All had things in common. All knew they had tried.
The thing the never realized . . . all of them would die.

That's the sad part of reality: Life stops on a dime.
They fought for peace and justice. But they simply ran out of time.

THE WALL WITH A PITFALL

There's a wall of freedom which holds many soldiers' names
Who fought for their beliefs and the values it contains.
They understood commitment and the value of human lives
And what it takes to be happy, faithful, true and wise.

And that same wall that keeps others from being free.
It holds them in bondage with pain and agony.
It is just a wall; yet it instills in loved ones grief and pain.
They return again and again knowing it's best
Not to complain.

A wall can be dangerous. It can be constructed and used
For good or evil. What did the builders believe?
If freedom is what you want, stay away from walls.

And remember when you climb walls
To remember the pitfalls.

SIXTY THOUSAND NAMES

We know The Freedom Wall, it holds sixty thousand names:
Men all lost in battle, no two the same.

Although they're individuals, collectively they're one.
They did a thankless job. They knew it must be done.

That was why the wall was built: To honor those who died.
So do that: Honor these soldiers who did much more than tried.

UNCLE JED

I was driving down the road and heard a voice call out:
Won't you stop and see me? We have a lot to talk about!

I stopped and looked around and, much to my dismay,
I saw it was Uncle Jed, whose final debt was paid.

"You were killed in battle fifty years ago."
"Why have you come back?" Jed, "I don't really know."

Maybe I've come to tell you why I had to die:
To protect you and the country where you now reside."

We talked about an hour. He told a tale or two –
What it meant to him and to the others that he knew.

Americans now deceased fought for a cause:
For freedom and liberty and, above all else, for our laws.

THE WALL

The Freedom Wall is symbolic of soldiers
Who fought in foreign wars
For liberty and freedom.
They were loyal to their cores!

Those who really care are far and few between.
The soldiers sacrificed their lives -
They knew just what it means:

They fought and stopped the evil.
We can stop it once again.
Yes, we can stop it someday,
Perhaps someday it will end!

THE DISAPPEARING MAN

A man was standing at the wall. He had a funny look.
He shook his head in wonder
And then he took out a leather book.

He read a while. He pondered. Something was on his mind. I walked
up to him and asked, "Who are you trying to find?"

He didn't answer right away. It seemed he didn't know.
Then he said to me, "This wall has a funny glow."
"A glow?" I asked. "What do you mean? It looks okay to me."
"Yes I know, for some it's impossible to see"

I thought, "What a kook! He is more than I can bear!"

I shook my head and walked away

But when I turned around, he had simply disappeared.

THE SOLDIER

I was sitting at my desk engaged in paperwork.
I was listening to some music on my iPod.
I thought I saw somebody walking toward me. He looked like a soldier. Oh, my God!

I asked him, "Where are you going?" He didn't speak a word. He just looked around and asked, "Where am I?" is what I heard

I told him, "You're in Palmdale, California - the USA."
That's when the soldier started to cry.
I heard a bomb explode.
And vanished completely in the night.

I got up and walked to where he had been standing. He'd disappeared into the Wall.
I wonder whenever I think about him–
That's answering freedom's call!

FREEDOM AND LIBERTY

If freedom and liberty were the only words we knew,
And love and understanding were for a precious few,
Then many would be living elsewhere as a fraud -
Without those words which mean so much to God.

But unfortunately we've had to pay for freedom
With human lives -
So many lost in battles . . .
It is tragedy in disguise!

The names exist deep within the Freedom Wall.
And freedom and liberty beckon to our call.

LIBERTY FOR EVERYONE

Liberty is for all of us, no matter our races or creeds.
Women, men, sons and daughters . . . we all have our needs.

We all want freedom, the chance to be ourselves:
To establish our identity, for selves, with everyone else.

Freedom is essential and should not be ignored.
Honor it; treasure it; peace and happiness are your reward.

No one can substitute it - it's yours for you to take.
And protect it forever, for our nation's sake.

THE WALL WILL LAST

The Wall will last forever, at least in people's minds.
You can't erase the memory made from tears of time.

People won't forget
It stands for all to see.

That's why the Wall stands for
A country that is free!

Many soldiers died, so we can be free to live
In a democracy that's willing to forgive.

So here's an invitation: Come to the Wall!
The Wall will last forever; for one and all!

CHRISTMAS POEMS

SANTA?

Is there really a Santa Claus?

Do You believe in Christmas, and in dreams?

Santa is a wisp of your imagination very much alive and doing well, if you feel alive when you give someone a present, then yes there is a Santa Claus, who will give you a spiritual gift and send you into an imaginary realm. Santa is a desire to make someone happy, to give from the bottom of your heart So, through these poems I give a fantasy journey and say Merry Christmas and Ho Ho Ho...

Bruce Robertson

RUDOLPH, RUDOLPH

Rudolph, Rudolph! Time to wake!
You must get up for goodness sake.
Santa's got a job for you.
You're the one to see it through.

Rudolph groaned. Please go away!
Why must I pull his sleigh?
Why must I every time this year
Have to be his lead reindeer?

Come on Rudolph! You shouldn't pout!
It's an honor to help him out!
After all, you are his friend.
So get him there and back again!

Oh no! No, not me!
That ain't the way it should be!
I'd rather sleep the night away
Than to pull his heavy sleigh!

Santa's elves just shook their heads,
They couldn't believe what Rudolph said.
He'd rather sleep the night away
Than help Santa with his sleigh.

Rudolph thought, golly gee!
What's come over me?
It's only once a year.
I'll be Santa's lead reindeer!

Up, up and away they flew.
Santa and you know who –
Over cities far and near,
Back home for another year.

I'M PROUD

Santa's sleigh is about to land
With Rudolph in the lead.
Santa knows without him,
He'd probably not succeed.

He's very proud of Rudolph
And all his reindeer
Making it much easier
Each and every year.

Rudolph, I'm proud of you
With all you have done:
Helping me deliver gifts
For each and everyone.

And Donner, Blitzen, Comet,
To me you're the best!
Now it's time for all of us
To take a winters rest.

It isn't very often
Santa Feels this way.
For all that he's been through
To prepare for Christmas Day.

But now it's time for him
And all Santa's crew
To finish off the night
The way they always do.

SANTA'S FAST ASLEEP

Santa's fast asleep –
Cozy in his bed.
Santa's elves have all gone home.
The reindeer have been fed.

He's tired and he's weak
I guess that's what comes with time.
Now he's fast asleep
With nothing on his mind.

Mrs. Claus is proud
Of all the things he's done –
Giving Christmas gifts
To each and everyone.

And when it's time for Santa
To let his slumber end,
You know that Santa will rise
And do it all again.

SANTA SNORES!

I find really funny!
It tickles me to the core!
Someone told me yesterday
That Santa Really snores

My resource is reliable.
I've used her once or twice.
Do you know who told me?
It was Santa's wife!

I shook my head in wonder.
I was laughing all the while!
I don't know why she told me.
It tends to make me smile.

She said, "I really love him.
But how much can I take?
When he goes to sleep,
He keeps me wide awake."

SANTA'S SURPRISE

Santa looked out the window
And what did we see?
A motorcycle!
As red as can be.

He asked "whose bike?"
And to his surprise, It's yours, Santa
For being so nice.

Santa choked up!
For me, are you sure?
Yes, Dear Santa,
And much more!

A years' worth of gas
Free as it can be…
All of this for
Little ole me?

I don't know what to say!
I'm Aghast!
Mrs. Claus says
"I know it won't last"

Oh one more thing:
Don't forget
You can't ride the bike
Without a helmet

Now Santa rides around
As happy as can be!
Ho ho ho!
Merry Christmas to me!

Where's Rudolph

Santa can't believe it, Rudolph ran away?
Why? I don't understand, he was fine yesterday.
Was it something I said, that got him so upset?
If it was I can't recall, sometimes I forget.

Maybe I'll wait a while, maybe he'll come back,
Everybody misses him; he keeps us all on track.
What would we do without him?
He's loyal to the end.

Since he changed his attitude
He's been a loyal friend
It isn't like him to disappear,
We don't know why, but then.....

We're not really worried, he'll be back again
And when he does we'll ask him
Why did you run away?
Was it something that was said,
Or was it Santa's sleigh?

Runaway Deer!

Santa's having trouble sleeping, Rudolph's on his mind.
Where'd he run off to, he can't be hard to find.
If he's not back by morning, we are going to have to try.
If we can't find him, kiss this trip good bye.

We'll find another reindeer, with a shiny nose.
What's the odds on that, one that somehow glows.
If we can't find him we will have to do without,
We've done it before Rudolph, we're spoiled without a doubt.

What's that on the horizon? Someone coming strong,
It sure looks like Rudolph, I pray I'm not wrong.
Oh my God, it's him, as live as he can be.
Welcome back Rudolph, to your family.

Christmas Greetings

It's a task unsurmountable, Santa does each year,
It's one he does willingly, bringing Christmas cheer.
Gifts made with loving hands with children on their minds,
Some will last forever, from memories left behind.

Generations following will inherit yesterday,
Bringing to the children gifts upon his sleigh.
Singing carols and laughing, underneath the Christmas tree,
That's what the season's all about,
Gifts for you and me.

CHRISTMAS AGAIN

He doesn't have to hurry
Time is on his side.
The fishing hole is handy,
A perfect place to hide

He knows he can take his time
He'll gradually reach his goal
A little at a time
Till the season takes a toll.

For when the time arrives
For him to stretch and bend.
Christmas will be near
And he'll do it all again

A VERY SPECIAL MOMENT

It was a very special moment
When he saw Rudolph's nose!
I can't believe my eyes, he said!
It glows wherever he goes!

It's a little flashlight in the dark!
It glows where it might be!
I've got to have him pull my sleigh!
It means that much to me!

Santa said, "Now listen –
Its only once a year."
Rudolph said, "Dear Santa,
I'll be your lead reindeer.

KEEPING CHRISTMAS CHRISTMAS

He knows it's quite a while
For Christmas to arrive.
Santa knows what to do
To keep Christmas alive.

Just to keep up the spirits
Of everyone around
Working energetically
So kids won't be let down.

He doesn't overdo it,
He takes a break or two.
He may even go fishing,
That's what he likes to do.

And as for the Christmas holiday,
That sometimes may be rough.
Well Christmas comes once a year,
And that's soon enough.

THE CHRISTMAS TREE

When I was only four years old,
I loved our Christmas tree.
I knew the presents under it,
Were mostly there for me.

I'd imagine what they really were
As children usually do.
All were different toys
That I could rummage through

My mommy and my daddy told me,
Santa put them there.
And I believe he really did.
Who else could be so fair?

Everybody got a gift!
That's the way it should be,
Gifts scattered all about,
Underneath the Christmas tree.

Santa Being Santa

Santa being Santa, knows a lot of folk,
Movie stars, celebrities, and a lot of silly jokes.
But when it comes to children, there's a different way.
No one puts his children down, or puts them on display.

Santa is extravagant, when it comes to his kids.
He protects them in every way, like his mother did.
She protected him from evil the very best she could, That's what makes him who he is, and why he is so good.

Santa being Santa loves his elves and reindeer too,
Willing to be a part of what he's trying to do.
Being a servant to his kids on Christmas Eve,
Recipients of compassion, to all who still believe.

Arnie

Santa can't believe it, his shops a total mess.
Toys are scattered everywhere, what happened here is just a guess.
Why would his elves leave so disarrayed?
It shows no respect for what they do each day.

All at once he realized, all of them are gone,
Not an elf anywhere, he knows somethings wrong.
He looks for them high and low calling out their names,
No one answers Santa, he's about to go insane.

Then he sees note on a bench off to the rear.
It reads:
Santa, your elves are all in fear,
Don't try to find them, you can't cause there's a hitch.
If you do you'll be sorry
Signed, your friend, The Grinch

Now Santa understands, there's a task to be done,
It involves Arnie, his magic elf, he'll help anyone
He contacts Arnie and says, "Here's what I say, the elves have been kidnapped by the Grinch this Christmas day. I need your help Arnie, this is an emergency."
Arnie calls him back, "You can count on me."

A few hours later, a knock upon the door,
All fifty elves are back, home once more.

Arnie, you're amazing, how you did it, I'll not ask.
I thank you for all you've done, you completed it so fast.
Arnie just smiled and said, "I just sit here up on the shelf,
That's why they call me

Arnie the Magic Elf.

Lessons

Santa's taking lessons, learning how to ski
He says it's good exercise, it will make a man of me.
I'll go down around the slopes, around my favorite bend
That's the easy part, not going up again.

Santa's taking lessons in another sport,
Not bowling, or checkers, or on the tennis court
What Santa's trying to do, that's worth his time?
Santa's trying very hard to learn how to climb.

Losing Weight

Santa's got a problem; he may have to skimp,
He's getting heavier; it's causing him to limp.
His weight is astronomical, three twenty when he weighed,
Mrs. Claus is concerned, Santa is afraid.

He doesn't want to diet; its way to much effort,
He needs his strength to do his job; it takes a lot of work.
There's got to be moderation if he should succeed,
Losing weight is hard to do, when you like to eat.

The elves are doing what they can to give him their support,
Keeping him away from the food court.
Mrs Claus is doing her best to put less on his plate,
That's the only way they know, to help Santa Claus lose weight.

Mrs. Clause

You know about Santa, Rudolph and the elves,
Santa delivers presents from the gifts upon the shelves.
But what about Mrs. Clause, she's important too.
She's the backbone of his success, she helps him see it through.

She gives him encouragement, keeps him on his toes.
Relaxes him now and then, when he's 'bout to explode.
Sets the pace for what he does, so it won't be routine, Soothes him every night, so his sleep will be serene.

Everyone's important, each in different ways,
That's what makes them what they are, a team put on display.
If it weren't for Mrs. Clause their endeavors would be lost.
That's why she's regarded and respected by the boss.

No Christmas!

Children everywhere are starting to believe,
This year Santa's feeling bad, there will be no Christmas Eve.
Christmas stockings hanging will be empty with despair, What will we do if Santa doesn't really care?

Well Santa cares a lot, it's hard for him to stray,
He's much like Rudolph, when he wouldn't pull his sleigh.
Every year he does this, it gets so routine,
He's expected once a year to gladly make the scene.

Well Rudolph talked to Santa, respectfully of course,
"Do you remember me when I was so remorse?"
I got my act together, you can do the same.
You always will be Santa that will never change."

Santa said to Rudolph, "You know, you're okay.
I can still deliver gifts on this Christmas Day.
You changed your way of thinking, I can do the same.
As long as I am Santa, Christmas will remain."

The Mission

Santa's on a mission that no one knows about,
It's a secret to him, he doesn't want it out.
No one knows what he is doing, that's the way it has to be.
Old Saint Nick is very good at creating mystery.

Th' elves take it real hard, why doesn't he confer?
After all we're friends, at least we once were.
How dare him be mysterious to the ones that really care.
Even Mrs. Clause is left in the air.

Santa's coming back, with a package in his hand.
A smile upon his face, soon they'll understand.
He gathers them all around underneath the Christmas tree.
A present for Mrs. Clause, Happy Anniversary.

Ready To Deliver

It won't be long till Christmas, Just a day away,
The elves have done the maintenance on the ol' man's sleigh.
Everything is ready, the packages are wrapped,
All that's left is loading then Santa can relax.

Santa's taking inventory, checking his list;
A train set for Bobby and a baby doll for sis.
The reindeer and Rudolph are ready to fly,
That is what they're waiting for, Christmas to arrive.

The night of Christmas is just one day away,
Santa's trying to unwind, settle down for Christmas Day.
When the time arrives to deliver all the toys,
He'll be ready to do his thing for the girls and boys.

Santa's Glasses

I remember a time when Santa needed glasses,
it was hard to read his mail.

It got worse as time went by,
when his eyesight began to fail.

So he bought a pair to see,
maybe his vision would improve.

And to his surprise he could see,
now Santa's in the groove.

He could see so much better,
he could read and he could write.
That's what glasses do,
they improve his eye sight.

Santa's Everywhere!

Mommy and Billy went to the mall to buy a gift or two,
Billy looked at mom, "can I ask something of you?"
Go ahead Billy, I know how much you care,
"How many Santa's are there, they are everywhere."

Mommy looked at Billy, smiled with Christmas cheer,
They are Santa's helpers, they do this every year.
Billy said to mommy. I know there's only one,
'Cause Santa can't be everywhere, that wouldn't be much fun.

Santa's Getting Old

Santa's pushing 500 years,
time's beginning to take it's toll.
He's not doing what he used to do,
he's really getting slow.

That's where the elves come in,
they take up the slack.
They are happy to be helping him,
they make up what he lacks.

Rudolph and the reindeer
do the best they can.
They carry him from house to house,
he's a very heavy man.
And when he's done delivering
to every nook and bend,
They have to take him back
to his home again.

They don't mind doing it,
he's special in every way.
From the elves and Rudolph
up to Santa's sleigh.

And above all else Mrs. Clause
who knows how to treat her man.
At five hundred Santa needs a helping hand.

The Brotherhood

Santa sent a note, thanking him again.
What you did for us, no one can contend.
You are a vital part of what we do each year.
You are asking you to join us, not as a volunteer.

(Arnie replies) All of you are special, individually and whole.
I'd love to be part of you, why I can't, I've no control.
I'm now part of a brotherhood to defend folks like you.
The society of magic elves, who do what we do.

I have a special gift, I hope you can accept,
Honorary elves of magic intent.
You will have my magic for just a little while,
Merry Christmas all of you with a twinkle and a smile.

The Letter

Santa received a letter from a boy named Dell,
Daddy left us years ago, and mommy isn't well.
I'm not asking for anything, I'm blessed with who I have.
A loving mom to hold me, when I'm feeling bad.

Mommy, she has cancer, not expected to live long.
Every second I'm with her, helps to keep her strong.
Please help me if you can, to make what's left worthwhile,
Maybe just a simple thing, that will make her smile.

Tears came from Santa's eyes,
what a wonderful boy,
He loves his mother with all his heart
and want to bring her joy.
She hasn't long to be here,
the little boy replies,
Please bring my mommy happiness,
before the day she dies.

The Christmas Party

Santa's going to throw a party, for all his elves and deer.
A Christmas party filled with gifts he has most every year.
Dancing girls, I don't think Mrs. Clause would allow.
That's okay with Santa, he didn't want them anyhow.

There'll be lots of presents, a Christmas carol or two.
A tree Santa pitched, accepted by his crew.
Decorations everywhere, to brighten up the night.
A Ho Ho Ho from Santa, and even Christmas lights.

Everything went perfect, everyone had a ball.
The punch was extra tasty, drank by one and all.
Even Mrs. Clause had a lot of fun,
Christmas is always special, for each and every one.

The Coffee Caper

Santa's excited, Christmas Eve this night
He can hardly wait for the time to pass by
He's got his presents ready to deliver Christmas Eve
Another cup of coffee to drink before he leaves

He's bouncing around the cottage like an energetic man,
Far beyond what's normal, doing what he can
He asks his elves with vigor, "Have the reindeer been fed?"
They respond yes, but why is your face so red?

Another cup of coffee, to get him on his way
Two more cups of coffee will complete Santa's day
One more cup of coffee, that's terribly extreme
That's your problem Santa, way too much caffeine

The Wall

Walls are built to keep people out, but not on Christmas Eve,
He delivers to everyone, even to those who don't believe.
He isn't partial in any way, when it comes to one and all
That's why Santa doesn't believe there should be a wall.

He wants peace another way to exist among man kind
He wants the Holy Spirit to intervene when your unkind
He wants Christmas everyday, to dwell in everyone.
He wants the spirit of giving, when freedoms truly won

That's why he really is, someone who really cares
Who exists in children's hearts, in dolls and Teddy Bears.
Who becomes a glimmer in the eyes of one and all,
The poor, the rich, the middle class who can tear down any wall

The Tooth Ache

Santa's got a tooth ache, he hasn't slept all night,
It's a problem a dentist could easily make right.
But Santa doesn't like dentists very much
He could suffer through the pain or do something in a rush.

He decides the latter, he calls Dr. Barge,
He says, "I need your services, how much do you charge?"
Normally five dollars, that is my normal fee,
But for you dear Santa, It's absolutely free.

Santa says, "I'll be there, I need your service now.
My tooth is killing me, can you get me in somehow?"
Come on in Santa, you're the only one
Now Santa is feeling better after all that has been done.

The Toast

Here's to everyone, th' elves and my reindeer,
Here's to Mrs. Clause, Who guides me every year.
Here's to the children, upon my Christmas list,
If it weren't for them I would not exist.

And here's to the Grinch, who shows me what I lack,
Who keeps me on my toes, so I can't relax.
If it weren't for him, my life would be a bore,
Here's to everybody, a new year and many more

Bruce Robertson

What about Santa

Every year come Christmas Eve, Santa loads his sleigh,
Filled with Christmas goodies for children Christmas day.
Just knowing they are happy gives the man a kick,
But what about Santa, what does he get?

No one gives him anything, not even a thought,
They're too busy playing with the toys he brought.
Santa's just a memory of the coming year,
Then he does it all again, when Christmas time is near.

Where Have You Been

Rudolph, where have you been? Why did you run away?
Was it something I said that made you act that way?
No Santa, it's nothing that you said to me,
I had to get away, to gain some energy.

You see I've been listless, I really don't know why.
I know it can't be physical, but all I do is cry.
But now that I am back, I know what's going on.
This is where I need to be, that's why I was gone.

Two Bosom Buddies

Santa and I are buddies, that's what I like to think.
What Santa says I listen, with him it's swim or sink.
I'd rather do whatever he says, it's much easier that way.
From Rudolf, Comet, Blitzen; the ones who pull his sleigh

Santa read the letter, his reindeer wrote him.
He has mixed emotions, they wrote it on a whim.
Rudolph was the master mind, of this little quote.
Its something he thought of as a stupid little joke.

Santa now is laughing, at the letter that he read.
Rudolph and I are buddies, what more can be said.
I guess that is the way it is between bosom pals,
Rudolph with is red nose and Santa with his elves.

Christmas Morning

When you wake up Christmas morning and stumble to the tree,
You wonder where they came from, are there any for me?
I guess that is normal of a child of four,
When you open one and ask, "are there any more?"

Then you ask mommy, "who put them there?"
Mommy answers "Santa, who else could be so fair?"
Everybody got a gift from Santa Clause last night,
That's what Christmas is all about, doing what is right.

The Bible

There are many books that will harm you, I know one that won't.
That one is called the Bible, some read it, some don't.
The Bible should be cherished, and held next to the heart.
It will guide you when you're feeling bad, and calm you when it's dark.

It can tell you of his wondrous love in many different ways.
How Jesus sacrifices his life, and the reason you should pray.
It will walk you through adversity, and set your mind at ease.
And most of all show, how easy He is to please.

The Bible is th' only book that can lift you when you're down.
And if you're lost the Bible can tell you you've been found.
So pick it up and read it, that's all you have to do.
And God will bless you every day, by giving back to you.

www.ingramcontent.com/pod-product-compliance
Lightning Source LLC
LaVergne TN
LVHW041540060526
838200LV00037B/1066